Death Is A Dancer

Jessica Marrone

BookLeaf
Publishing

India | USA | UK

Death Is A Dancer © 2024 Jessica Marrone

All rights reserved.

Presentation by *BookLeaf Publishing*

Web: www.bookleafpub.com

E-mail: info@bookleafpub.com

ISBN: 9789360940638

First edition 2024

This collection is dedicated to my Grandma, my dear friend Jake, and my beloved Bailey who are no longer with me, but inspired this endeavor. You are always in my heart.

PREFACE

At the end of 2023 as the New Year was about to ring, I stumbled upon an advertisement for a writing challenge. Write 21 poems in 21 days. I wondered if this feat would be possible for me. I hadn't written a poem in what has felt like years. Deciding that I needed to challenge myself, I signed up and began pondering what overarching theme I wanted to explore.

It didn't take long for me to settle upon Death. It's an inescapable part of life. Always looming somewhere off in the distance. Always waiting for us. Sometimes it comes too early.

It stirs so many emotions in us, doesn't it? Anger at the loss of losing someone we love. Fear for what happens to us when we die. Is there something after this? There's also the beauty in life springing forth from death. A tree dies and it provides warmth for a family seeking shelter. There's compassion from workers in the death industry who treat our loved ones with respect until the very end. There is finally the acceptance that Death walks among us and we realize we must live every day to its fullest.

I felt truly inspired when I began exploring all of the facets of Death and digging into the different narratives I could express. I allowed myself to step into the shoes of others in order to see Death from their eyes. I took pause and reflected from my own pain and immortalized my own feelings in several poems for the loved ones I've lost too soon.

This experience has caused me to reflect on my own thoughts about Death and that age old question of what lies beyond our realm of possibility. I strived to make this poetry collection a mixture of pain and beauty. It's impossible to discuss the topic of Death without getting a bit sad, but it is my hope that as you read through these poems, you will not only feel sad but love, nostalgia, joy, peace, and maybe a giggle or two.

Lastly, I want to thank you for purchasing this collection. I have wanted to be a published author for many years, and I am proud to say that this collection is my first publication, giving me that long sought after title of "Published Author." Thank you to everyone who has supported my dreams to becoming an author that tells the story I want to tell, namely: my parents, Steve and Brandie, my best friends Megan and

Nancy, and my grandparents Joe Sr. and Jo Anna. Thank you for encouraging me to pursue my creativity and helping me find my confidence to put my work out there for the world. I love you all.

Mr. Reaper's House Call

The Reaper knocked on my door
"If you please, I have room for one more."
"I'm sorry, sir, there's been a mistake," I said,
"For you see, I much rather not be dead."
I grabbed his bony hand and flashed a smile
"Now won't you come in and sit for a while?"
He gazed at me with such bewilderment.
Would he partake in my fantastical merriment?
Sure enough Mr. Reaper spoke with me until dawn
Then he said "I simply must be heading on,
Twenty more souls I must take back
But thank you for showing me the compassion I
lack."
It was then that I awoke from my slumber
Thankful that today was not my number.
Last night I charmed the Reaper
He said my soul was quite the keeper.

Ages

0 - How does this living thing go?

1 - Now I'm starting to have fun!

2 - Why am I always so blue?

3 - Ha ha! Can't control me!

4 - Why doesn't Santa use the door?

5 - Dad, look at this worm! It's still alive.

6 - Let's play Pick Up Sticks!

7 - It's hard without training wheels but I'll try again.

8 - I didn't mean to break that plate.

9 - You mean, this puppy is all mine?

10 - I made a pillow fort in the den.

11 - What's Seven Minutes in Heaven?

12 - My body's changing, but let's not delve.

13 - Finally! No longer a tween!

14 - Why are middle schoolers so mean?

15 - Sorry, my mom said I have to clean.

16 - My style's called "scene".

17 - We kissed under the cinema screen!

18 - I feel so in-between.

19 - I decorated my dorm in green.

20 - I'll see you on Rainbow Bridge where the squirrels are aplenty.

21 - Don't worry, I'll just drink one.

22 - I forgot that paper was due.

23 - Wow, I got my degree!

24 - She said yes to forevermore!

25 - So now I can rent a car to drive?

26 - Why's there so much in this house to fix?

27 - Time to vote for the next Congressmen.

28 - She's two weeks late.

29 - I can't believe this little girl is mine.

30 - Well isn't she feeling flirty.

31 - Oh my god, I'm having a son!

33 - My job finally promoted me!

34 - So many bills. How many more?

35 - How am I supposed to keep this wild child alive?

36 - I'm cleaning up all her Pick Up Sticks.

37 - Son, wait until Grandpa says "amen".

38 - Oh no, one day she's going to be ready to date.

39 - How'd we end up with this random feline?

40 - Should I get a car that's a little more sporty?

41 - Nice job, son! That's how a touchdown is done!

42 - Mom, what am I supposed to do without you?

43 - She's got a crush. Who is he?

44 - Could've sworn there was more hair up there before.

45 - I regret teaching her how to drive.

46 - This company is up to old tricks.

47 - Well, time to find a job again.

48 - I can't believe he's going to graduate.

49 - His commanding officer says he's doing just fine.

50 - Half a decade, isn't that nifty?

51 - My morning jog used to be more fun.

52 - But, she's too young to say "I do."

53 - Well, honey, now it's just you and me.

54 - I'd retire now, but I'd be poor.

55 - I'm grateful to be alive.

56 - It's going to be a girl, she predicts.

57 - Well, it's a boy. Our family has more men.

58 - I need to watch my weight.

59 - The results came back benign.

60 - Another year! Thank the stars over Dixie!

61 - He's coming home, the war's been won.

62 - Here, let Grandpa tie your shoe.

63 - So much of the world I've left to see.

64 - Thanks for the watch! I'm out the door.

65 - I love watching my family thrive.

66 - Taking stock of how the clock always ticks

67 - Always thinking back to way back when

68 - I'm starting to not feel so great.

69 - My body hurts, but trust me I'm fine.

70 - If only I could feel like I did when I was twenty.

71 - I think my time is almost done.

72 - And now I say goodbye to you.

Decay

Bones in the forest
Sacrifice themselves today
For tomorrow's rose

Cardinal

You left me too soon
And I hate you for it.

Was my love not enough
To keep you with me?
Did I do something
That made you go away?

I'm sorry for what I said
Just please come back.
Please.

You're gone and I hate you.

You weren't supposed to leave.
Were my prayers not strong enough?
Was I not good enough?

Did you hate me?
Because I hate you

You needed to stick around
To watch me grow up.

No, I don't want your photographs.
I don't want your trinkets.
I don't want your voice on a tape.

I don't want your obituary clipped from the
newspaper.
I don't want the cardinal outside my window.

I just want you.

And I hate you for not being here
And for not telling me "goodbye"
And myself for not fighting harder to make you stay.

But mostly I just hate how much I miss you.

You couldn't even give me "goodbye"
Without a whisper you were just gone

So now I have to settle for the photographs
And the trinkets on the mantle
Your laughter on a tape
The flowers from your grave
And the cardinal perched outside my window.

7

Death Is A Dancer

I wanted to keep on being
So when Death came a-callin' for me
I asked him if he knew the Swing.
He lay down his scythe
Grabbed my hand with his carpals
And I prepared for the dance of my life.

I hummed the tune frolicking in my head
Death followed along in a one-two step
This was much better than being dead.
But I tripped over my two left feet.
He sighed, dropped my hands, and reached for his
scythe
"Wait!" I yelled, not ready to admit defeat.

"Do you know the Tango?"
He nodded under his dark cloak
"Well then let's go, sway me to and fro!"
I pulled myself close to his bones, oh what a chill!
"My goodness, my friend! You're so cold!"
But my shivers couldn't pull me away from this thrill.

He was quite good and could cha cha all night long
So we tapped and twisted and dipped under the stars.
It's funny, neither of us felt quite bothered by the lack
of song.
Death pulled me close and began a foxtrot
To be honest, I delighted seeing him having fun

If nothing else, it was better than to rot.

If he had eyes under his hood, I bet they were aglow
The way he gallivanted across my hospital room
He simply couldn't wait to show off his Bolero
The momentum continued with a waltz
I had to stop had to end the dancing
The pain in my chest, I admit, is one of my faults.

"I'm so sorry to ruin your fun"
Death dropped my hands and bowed his head
"I know. We both know my time is done."
He grabbed his scythe and looked in my eyes.
"Just please, promise me it won't hurt."
It's a good thing I already said my goodbyes.

He threw his scythe down and started a jive.
So with a giggle, I shimmied in my dressing gown
I suppose it was one last moment to feel alive.
Grabbing his cloak, I held Death close and felt all of
his bone
"I'm glad to have had this dance," I hugged him tight.
It's wonderful that for a night, neither of us felt so
alone.

A Kind Message To Ghost Hunters

The floorboards are a-rattlin'
And the cats are a-chatterin'
Must be time for the ghosts to come a-playin'

A cold breeze fills the room
And you're tempted by the ghastly doom
But it's just the spirits comin' to call

The cupboards are a-shakin'
I can see you're over there a-quakin'
He and his friends ain't mean you no harm

See, just about this time er' night
The dead come back to my delight
Celebratin' that witchin' hour with some old friends

The kitchen lights are a-flickerin'
Don't worry, he and the missus are just bickerin'
She done told him she hate this wallpaper

My ghoulish friends ain't understandin'
That times do be a-changin'
And now this ol' farmhouse is mine

Now, I don't really mind sharin'
Since their souls do still be carin'

But can't y'all help with the washin' a night or two?

Yeah sometimes they're loud
And it attracts some of the wrong crowd
Aways comin' by tryin' to tell 'em "hi"

That's where my friends and I get along.
Sometimes y'all hunters be gettin' it wrong
They just wanna find some peace

Y'all come 'round here with those ouija boards
Drawin' spectators out here in hordes
Ain't no better than the paparazzi

My friends like to dance in the air
After losin' their lives, I think that's fair
Just let 'em be until sunrise when they go back to bed

One day that's gonna be you and me
Then you'll think "damn won't they let me be?"
Give 'em some space, and let 'em come a-playin'

3 A.M. Thoughts

He stopped by my cubicle and asked
"How's it going?"

And for a moment I paused
Does he want honesty?

That at 3 a.m. I was consumed in a cold sweat
Tightness in my chest unable to breathe

From thinking about the Infinity of it all
Knowing one day this will be over

And that I'll cease to exist
So will he and so will his kids and their kids

Wondering if it'll hurt and if I'll be ready for it
Or what's on the other side?

Is there another side or is this all there is?
Will I be forgotten as a surname on a stone?

But what if I burn because I didn't believe in the right
god?
Is it better to live again in Hell than to be nothing?

And if I do make it to Heaven, it's going to be so
boring

I mean, how can I live a perfect day over and over
and over?

And over and over and over
Until I'm ready for the cycle to end

When I'm wishing that it was just nothingness
So then maybe I'll find some peace

But instead, I just shrug and smile
"Oh you know, just livin' the dream."

The Tarot Card

I went to see the Medium the other day
Because I was worried my husband went astray.
She pulled the Death card from her tarot deck
Indeed, our marriage he did wreck.
Now the jury has sentenced my life away.

A Slasher's Lament

Why do they always have to run?
Of course you're going to trip
It's midnight
And you're barefoot in the woods
Obviously you're going to fall
And then I'll catch up
And then you'll start screaming
Jesus, I thought this was supposed to be fun.

Look, I only get 90 minutes to make my mark.
They don't care about your backstory
So save us all the exposition. Please.
Big deal, your parents are dead.
You will be soon too
If these heavy boots stop slowing me down
Wow. You just had to jump into the ocean
So now my kill goes to that damn shark!

Maybe I'd be better at this if I was a bit more scary
But the boys in masks wield a knife and machete.
Honestly you should consider yourself lucky
That I don't carry a balloon.
Sure, the clowns have all the fun
But let's be honest here
Neither of us want to be in the sewer.
And I don't even get me started on Carrie.

You know, maybe you should be a tad more grateful

I don't attack you while you're naked in the shower.
And I definitely don't wear Mommy's clothes.
I value your privacy
That's why I don't invade your dreams
So really, I should be saying "you're welcome"
And as I let you put up a fight for a dignified death
How about being a little thankful?

Would it be better if we played a game?
I didn't file the patents in time
So my machines will have to wait
How am I supposed to find the time?
All this tracking and hacking and somehow still
slacking
How's that damn doll got a bigger franchise than me?
He's 2 feet tall and ginger
Seriously, who's giving him all this fame?

Sorry, where were we now?
Oh yes, you're breaking all my rules.
God, you teenagers never learn or listen!
How many times does the creepy old man have to tell
you
To stay out of the abandoned house?
You brought this on yourselves
And it's so hard to be sympathetic
Your stupidity knows no bounds. How?!

Now cue the music and the thunder.
We're ready for the finale
So try to make it a good one
After all, I did save you for last

On the off chance there's a sequel.
But you're certainly no Ripley or Laurie
Or Sidney or any of Craven's Mambo No. 5
Still, you're too pretty to be put 6 feet under

Well, now that's that and you get the gist.
Oh come on! What are you doing?
Did you really have to scream
So melodramatically for 37 seconds?
Like your death scene is an Oscar contender?
Just fall down and die. You're embarrassing me.
Ugh, great. Thanks a lot, Victim #34.
That just put me on the B list.

Epitaph For A Friend

Here lies my beloved friend
And all the inside jokes we would quote
He was much too young for this to be his end
All I can do is speculate because he didn't leave
a note

I Wonder What The Angels Think

I wonder what the Angels think
When I choke on an olive
Or when I pick up my keys after one too many drinks
Do they breathe a sigh of relief?
When I trip over the sidewalk
Or when I board a plane
Do they rejoice at another crisis averted?

I wonder what the Angels think
When they give a stranger the Heimlich
Or when they tell a friend to crash at their place
Is it just what they're supposed to do?
When a cab driver shouts "watch your step!"
Or when the flight attendant helps with the oxygen
mask
Sometimes I wonder, "Could it be one of them?"

I wonder what the Angels think
When they look at us fragile little things
Or when they're told it's our time to go
Do they get sad they can't do more?
When they can't stop the consequences of our actions
Or when old age carries us off to the stars
Do they say a little prayer and hope we find our
peace?

Dreamcatcher

I found your dreamcatcher the other day
While exploring your old trinkets in the attic.
Granddaddy told us to look through your things.
I didn't want to pillage your dishes
Or rummage through your glassware.
But under some crumpled up newspaper
I saw a glimmer of brown feathers and beads.
He said it was yours and that I could take it home.
I hope that you don't mind if I borrow it.
You see, twenty-two years still feels like just one day
And I wanted something special to keep you close.
Back then I couldn't understand it all.
Just a little girl that couldn't comprehend cancer
And how you fought so hard but lost the battle.
Now I've grown, but I still have nightmares.
Sleep isn't so easy when you're not here
To help chase the monsters away
From the movie I was too young to watch
But I insisted I would be fine.
Sometimes I see a cardinal and I know it's you.
Dad's been showing me old photographs he found of
you as a girl.
I see a lot of myself in you, Grandma
But I wish I had more pictures of us together
A way to capture those short eight years we shared
Or to hear your voice before it's lost to me forever.
My memory isn't as crisp as it used to be

And I fear one day I'll truly lose all of you that I've
got left.
But at least I won't lose you tonight as I sleep
With your dreamcatcher watching over me,
Stealing away all the monsters from my bed
After living a movie I was much too young to see.

A Moth's Ode To A Caterpillar

To the humble Caterpillar whom gave his precious
life
Honoring nature's most sacred oath with his selfless
offering
May we never again endure hardship nor strife
By soaring to moonlit heavens on gilded wing.

Making Plans

I want neon lights and a disco ball
And my favorite music blaring down the hall.

Hand everyone packets of seeds
I don't want flowers that'll turn into weeds!

Don't play a boring, sad song
And don't make the service quite so long.

Pick a photo where I'm young and hot
And then another when I'm very clearly not.

Dress me in sequins and glitter on my lips.
Tell the Mortician no need to shave below my hips.

Prop me up in my special Death Day hat
It's all about me, so let's celebrate that!

Please recite all of my favorite jokes
If I go before my ex, tell him I hope he chokes.

Hold my service during the work week
Tell your boss you're busy mourning an antique

And if you need an excuse to be wrote
Don't worry, I already signed your Plague Doctor's
Note!

If I should die on a holiday weekend
Put me on ice before phoning my friend

And wear your favorite party clothes.
I don't care if you show up looking like hoes.

I want dancing, laughter and reminiscing, you see.
Just because I'm dead doesn't mean my party has to be!

Try not to cry, I lived a really great life.
Plus, I was also a super hot ex-wife.

Remember me as I once was
And maybe smile for me just because.

I'm definitely off to greener grass.
Tell my haters they can kiss my ass.

Give me one last roast before I'm toast
And leave thinking "wow, she's a great host."

Scatter my ashes under the stars when it's done.
See, now who said funerals can't be fun?

Coward's Curse

The other day, I came across a genie
Who told me he'd grant me wishes three
So on my first wish I asked for immortality
Because there's so much of the world I'm dying to
see.

He warned me "Be careful what you wish for
Once it's done, you cannot go back to before"
But of this scolding, I did not want to hear anymore
I was ready to venture out and explore.

At first the early years were extraordinarily fun
Living without the fears of coming undone
Soaking up that beautiful Antarctic sun
Celebrating all of the medals I had won.

Until the years turned to centuries unknown
And everyone I've ever loved has left me alone
Watching all of my children become grown
Burying my descendants is a pain I've never shone.

Every corner of the earth I had seen
A thousand times over, it became routine
But the genie was adamant he would not intervene
And reminds me none of this was unforeseen.

There was no more pleasure in earthly delights
I couldn't tell you when the days turned to nights

Or how many times I jumped from impressive
heights
Because I was finally ready for heavenly sights.

"You wanted more time, I warned you it would be
bad"
The genie told me, caring not that I was sad.
If anything, it sounded like the genie was a bit glad
To finally see the impact his words now had.

"I call it the Coward's Curse," he did state
"When your kind tries to defy its mortal fate
Always seeking out for something great
Until everything you want is behind a pearly gate."

My fear of what happens to us at the end
Was too much for my mind to ever comprehend
So now to all of you I will always transcend
Because the afterlife's a party I can never attend.

For All The Ones I Could Not Save

For all the ones I could not save
And to the families I feel I did betray
This pain I shall carry with me to my grave.

Your forgiveness I sincerely crave
But the words "I'm sorry" can hardly convey
This pain I shall carry with me to my grave.

There are souls who needed more than what I gave.
All I can do now is kneel down and pray
For all the ones I could not save.

Sometimes I can't make the science behave
And sometimes it won't take the maliaise away.
This pain I shall carry with me to my grave.

Please don't praise me or rave
Because I cry at the end of the day
For all the ones I could not save.

I try my best to be strong and brave
But heavy on my conscious does it weigh,
This pain I shall carry with me to my grave
For all the ones I could not save.

Spa Day

If you're looking for a new face
You have come to the right place.
It'll be a lovely spa day for you.
Oh goodness, we have so much to do!
I promise you'll leave here with nary a hair out of
place.

You don't talk much, and that's okay
I'm used to talking to myself all day.
Now let's get you bathed and clean
So you can step out on the scene.
I want your spirit to come out and play.

Most people don't think I'm very cool.
Because I flunked out of beauty school
I never could get the makeup quite right
The live ones put up too much of a fight
That's why I'm here, hanging out with a ghoul.

But rest assured. I mean it's all you can do
That I will take my best care of you
Because I'm the one who'll bring you back to life
If only for a moment so a husband can see his wife
Now I hope you don't mind that I use this glue.

At first, I didn't think I'd like working with the dead.
My friends said I should do something else instead
But, simply put, I like making people feel beautiful

Who cares about silly folks calling me delusional
It don't bother me none when I go to bed.

Now for the best part, adding color to your cheek.
In this photograph you look very meek.
I'll try to match your spirit as best I can
But we're lucky if you don't come out looking like a
man.
Oh that's just a joke to lighten up this dark week.

Let's add a pinky brown lipstick
To cover up how the sickness took you quick.
There! Now you look so very pretty
For all your loved ones to see
And some hairspray to make sure this 'do will stick.

I'm so sorry that we ended up meeting this way
But I hope you had a lovely last spa day
Let's put on your favorite blue dress
So you're ready to go out and impress.
Thank you so much for being my clay.

Regrets

Every day I sat
And waited for the rain
Only to discover
I missed so many sunny days.

Every day I held my breath
So I wouldn't smell the stench
Only to realize too late
I never smelled the roses.

Every day I minded my tongue
Because the silence was safe
Only to finally understand
My lips never whispered "I love you."

Every day I guarded my heart
So nobody could break it
Only to conclude now
At the end I am utterly alone.

Every day I stood still
Unable to move forward
But now I get it
As I'm on my way into the ground.

Paradise

Running across blades of grass so happily
And chasing after woodland creatures
In the glow of the warm summer rays
Never any thunderstorms to ruin my fun
But sometimes I prance through snow capped mountains
Or enjoy a nice nap by the flowing river
Where tranquil waterfalls lull me to sleep

Bursting with infectious energy amongst the clouds
Reveling in the heavenly delights surrounding us
Inside this paradise where I await you
Donning my fanciest collar and bows
Growing antsy watching you get older
Each and every day while I wait to greet you again.

Vampire Trees

I wish I was beautiful like the vampire trees
Green all year round because they never die.
And me? Well I'm only pretty in the spring
When my branches bear flowers
Or in autumn when my leaves glow red
But then my leaves turn ugly and brown.
They fall and leave me naked and decrepit,
Unlike the vampire trees standing proud
Adorned in fir and providing homes to the birds
Living eternally while all my beauty rests in peace.

But then one summer I felt a rope twist around my
branch.
A little girl swinging in a tire, giggling with delight
I looked to the vampire trees and the homes nestled in
them
Wondering why I couldn't live forever.
It's not fair that I shed and I die while
Vampire trees get invited inside where it's warm.
They dress in twinkling lights and shiny bobbles
Songs are sung about their beauty
And here I am, slowly dying each winter.

Another summer returns, and the little girl has grown.
Her friends take turns swinging and running around
my trunk.
I'm growing more brittle, but I muster my might

All to hear them giggle and play until the sunlight fades.
The little girl pats my bark and whispers "I love you"
Before running off in the twilight
And I hold my branches proud and high.

My little girl visits when the sun beams break
With a blanket under her arm and a book in her hand
Resting against my trunk I have to wonder
Of all the beautiful vampire trees
Why did she choose me?
"One day when I'm older, my daughter is going to use this swing"
She spoke to me as we enjoyed the forest songs.
If only I could tell her, I'm not a tree that lives forever,
She'll come back to find me cold and barren.

The little girl threw snowballs and took shelter behind my trunk
As her enemies decided to open fire against her.
I wish I had leaves to provide her cover in this great battle.
"What a bad hiding spot!" the tween assailant yelled.
"No, it's perfect!" my girl exclaimed.
"Because this is my favorite tree in all the forest!"
And she flung a cannonball of snow right at his face.
Is it true, my girl? That I am your favorite?
Even amongst all these magnificent vampire trees?

Years went by, and the little girl grew up.
Now her little girls play on her old swing

And her little boy climbs my branches.
"It's good to see you my old friend" she whispers to me,
I'm brittle now and ravaged by the storms
Branches have fallen and I'm so parched.
I had wanted to be something beautiful for so long
Only to end up forgotten by all in the end
Listening to the sounds of laughter one last time
Before the lumberjack comes to claim me.

"My darlings, let me tell you about this magnificent tree,"
My girl pulled her babies close and spoke softly.
"This tree stood for many years, growing big and tall,
Strong enough to hold me as I swung towards the skies,
Provided me shade when I read,
Sheltered me in my snowball fights,
Watched me grow up big and tall,
Showed me her blossoms and waited until I came home to show her mine."
She stroked my bark one last time to say goodbye.
"But now our friend's season has ended."

In all my moments, I wish now more than ever to be a vampire tree
I guess we're never ready for the end, are we?
"What will happen to your tree, Mama?"
A tiny hand gently tugged at my branch.
"Well, she's going to be cut down."
But why, the little blossoms wondered
Why not live forever like the vampire trees?

34

"This tree will become kindling to keep us warm at
night,
And logs to build our home to always protect us,
And paper in which your art and stories will be told
forever."

My girl must have known deep down in her heart
To live forever was always my most precious dream.
Now as the sun makes its evening departure
And my girl and her blossoms venture home
I look to the vampire trees and salute.
They will always be so beautiful in ways I could
never be,
Guardians of my lovely forest, taking care of the
creatures.
This life was good, but my destiny has changed
And perhaps now I can live forever too.

A Conversation With An Angel

She appeared to me as I wept in my bed
Humming beneath my dreamcatcher a familiar
lullaby
A vision of ethereal light, so soft and kind
"Why, dear sweet one, must you cry?"
As the warmth from her touch seeped within me
I sheepishly whispered "You would not understand."
But her humming beckoned me to confide
To all the secrets I kept locked inside my chest
"I'm so afraid that all I am is a dash."
She tilted her head and furrowed her wrinkleless
brow.
"Dear young one, may I ask what ever do you
mean?"
"See, I told you," I flung myself into my blanket and
yelled.
"We are all just a line on a rock, aren't we?"
The smallest of space etched into the stone
Underneath the immortal words "Here Lies"
"A name and two dates with a dash in the middle."
"I see what you mean now, dear sweet one,"
She brushed the hair from my face and whispered in
my ear
A heavenly secret she was sent to share to one who
might listen

"Your eyes see a scratch mark in stone, yes it might
be so
But, what is it that your heart sees?"
Tapping on the bed, she invited me to sit beside her
"My heart can't see anything, it's too dark."
"Then let me tell you what mine can see," she smiled.
"I can see a little girl taking her first steps
And the sound of her mother clapping with joy.
I can see a teenage girl blushing during her first date
And giggling when the handsome man kissed her
cheek.
I can see a young woman in a beautiful white dress
And her proud father trying desperately not to cry.
I can see a mother playing in the kitchen with her two
sons
And cheering in the stands at their high school
football games.
I can see a career woman who takes pride in her work
And a homemaker who loves welcoming anyone into
her home.
I see a grandmother who loves her three
grandchildren more than the world
And she cuddles her granddaughter when she's
frightened."
I wondered how she could see so much within a nick
in a piece of rock
A whole life of love and laughter existing in the
smallest of spaces.
Closing my eyes and opening my heart, I whispered
"I can see a grandmother wearing the blue dress I
picked out for her

And she's singing to me on the hammock in her backyard."
That's when I could finally see what the angel revealed to me
A line so small holds all the priceless treasures of the world
Taken from us much too soon or when it was that fated time
So long as we always remember to honor and cherish
Every smile, every laugh, every tear, every hug,
Every joke, every kiss, every touch, every moment.
Then we, too, can live forever inside a scratch in a stone.
And so I wiped my tears, while the angel caressed my back
Humming softly the lullaby she used to always sing to me.
As the early morning light crest upon the horizon
The angel melted away into a golden haze
Revealing a brilliant red cardinal on my window sill
Singing softly the lullaby she used to always sing.

Printed in the USA
CPSIA information can be obtained
at www.ICGtesting.com
LVHW020741230324
775007LV00012B/1214